THE VOID AND THE MOON

A COLLECTION OF POEMS

TUHINANSHU MISHRA

ISBN 979-888606537-4

This book has been published with all efforts taken to make the material error-free after the consent of the author. However, the author and the publisher do not assume and hereby disclaim any liability to any party for any loss, damage, or disruption caused by errors or omissions, whether such errors or omissions result from negligence, accident, or any other cause.

While every effort has been made to avoid any mistake or omission, this publication is being sold on the condition and understanding that neither the author nor the publishers or printers would be liable in any manner to any person by reason of any mistake or omission in this publication or for any action taken or omitted to be taken or advice rendered or accepted on the basis of this work. For any defect in printing or binding the publishers will be liable only to replace the defective copy by another copy of this work then available.

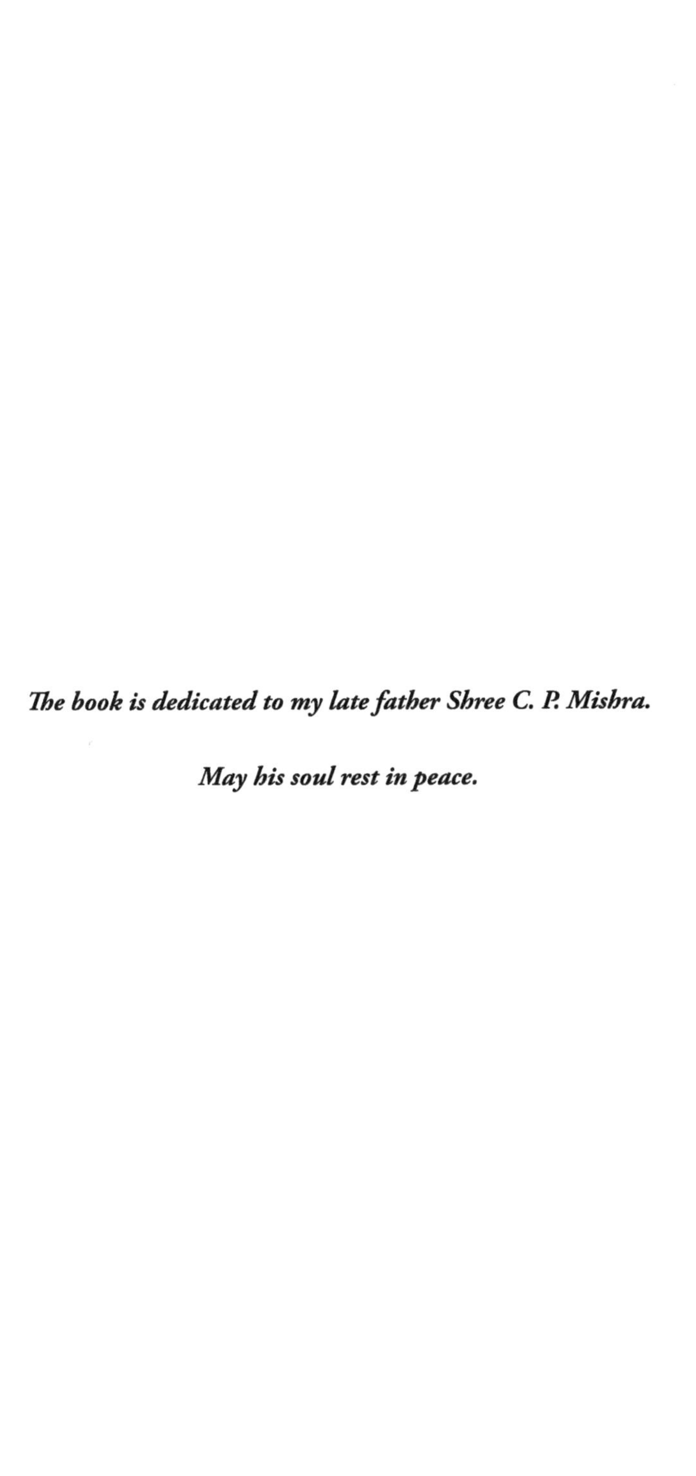

The book is dedicated to my late father Shree C. P. Mishra.

May his soul rest in peace.

Contents

Acknowledgements

The author is thankful to the almighty God, all his elders and friends for the support.

Thanks a bunch!

The Void and The Light

A void within the mind.
An absolute absence of thoughts.
Still the poetry continues,
for the soul is solely responsible,
for the words that emerge out,
and the mind is,
merely a dump of vocabulary,
merely a toolkit per se.
There sits the soul,
at the back of the stage,
driving the mind and body,
like trivial puppets,
dancing to the tune of instincts,
that lie within the core of the soul.
But why are words so crude ?
And the thoughts so bitter ?
Because the soul is,
scarred and tainted,
by the influence,
of a million other souls,
in this world,
each playing a part of its own,
in the theatre of the master puppeteer,

the one true light,
above all matter,
existential or not,
shinning so brightly,
that the form is,
incomprehensible,
and often misunderstood,
by each of these petty tainted souls,
whose entire triumph,
depends on the,
mind's void.

The Sword & The Shield

A wave of anger,
rose high above,
engulfing the shore of serenity,
where the mind was lying peacefully.
It blocked the sun,
which was granting enlightenment,
and terrified,
the birds of humour and wit.
The mind was hurled to a place afar,
where he found profound darkness.
He couldn't see for it was dark,
neither feel for it was secluded.
Lost alone in the wilderness,
he started developing fear,
of the unknown and unpredicted.
And then two fearsome hounds,
mania and phobia,
found his scent.
Thus, the chase began,
through peaks and gorges,
through days and nights.
Where shall he hide ?
Where shall he run ?

Tired of agony and pain,
he halted at a river,
of the power of will.
The Goddess of the river,
came rising above the sweet waters.
The mind begged for help,
but the Goddess spoke,
she would not indulge,
in the mind's battles.
But she would give him,
a fighting chance.
She drew a glistening sword,
called determination,
from under the waters,
and carved a shield called peace,
from a stone nearby.
She wished good luck and vanished.
The mind drew few breaths,
holding the sword in his hands.
And then he heard the growl,
of the two hungry hounds.
And before they could act,
the mind roared and pushed,
against their rock hard muzzles.
And it felt like days,

when the battle ended,
with the victory of the mind,
and the blood all around.
The Goddess appeared again,
smiling softly she said,
"You proved yourself worthy,
so you may keep the sword,
and ask a wish of your choice.
The mind asked the one thing,
that he longed for,
at that precise moment.
He asked her to grant him,
a small cozy cottage,
by the side of the river,
where he could live alone,
in silence.
The Goddess smiled,
and granted him his wish.
Since then the mind,
has been living in contentment,
with the shield of peace,
and the sword of determination.

The Wolf's Words

What does the wolf say,
when it howls to the full moon,
in the middle of the night?
Does it lament on the future?
On the long gaps,
of the upcoming days,
when the moon will be waning,
to nothingness?
Or does it just,
share all the forgotten tales,
that it was longing to tell,
all those times,
while the moon was away?
Whatever it is,
there are undeniable waves of passion,
filling the silent night sky,
in the long and damp howls.
And glory be to the quiet moon,
for she listens each story patiently,
while knowing deep within,
that this time of hers,
when she was in full vigor,
was limited by time,
and destiny.

The Elements

Four elements,
Water, air, fire and earth.
The river was thirsty for the ocean,
The air wanted to rule with the storm,
The spark wanted to reach great heights,
No one cared about civilisations.
Destruction and chaos everywhere.
Only the humble earth came forward,
to provide shelter to the lifeless.
And there's no surprise,
why humanity has always
trusted earth.

The Sparks

Sparks fell on water,
and their existence ceased.
They fell on wood,
and the entire forest caught fire.
The sparks were always pure.
It was always the fuel,
manipulating the fire,
on its own accord,
while blaming everything,
on the innocent sparks.

Intoxication

There is a certain intoxication,
in the air I am breathing,
for every progressive inhalation,
just increases my belief,
that you are,
somewhere nearby.
There is certain Intoxication,
in the morning sunshine,
for when I see it reflect,
in the morning dew,
I feel an unnecessary smile,
cutting across my lips.
There is an intoxication,
in the chirping of birds,
for my ears always perceive an optimism,
in their unfamiliar language.
There is definitely an intoxication,
in this very moment,
for I am absent-mindedly,
writing verses about you,
and your unknown existence,
in a stupid hope,
that maybe what I give to universe,

shall return to me,

in the form of a sophisticated yet soft hearted,

you.

Chills

A cold night
or a shivering breeze,
establishes differences.
Between a heart set aloof,
pledging purpose
and a heart surrounded by warmth,
of unconditional love.
Between a bar wench,
working night shifts
and a queen of the castle,
wrapped in blankets.
Between a hound of the dirty alley,
dying of painful hunger
and a cuddly hairy pup,
with a bowl of warm cereal.
But there's always a knight,
in these sad old tales,
who challenges his destiny,
with a grin on his face.
He has no disapproval,
to the bitterness of the chill,
and opens his arms,
to let his chest fill,

with all the savage stories,
and all the fatal histories,
that the cold wind carries,
residing in the winter's past memories.
For he is meant to sweat,
and surpass all expectations.
Even in the nights shall he tread,
overcoming all hesitations.

The Flow

Its easy,
to let it all go.
Let it go with the flow,
for the flow is older than time.
It is the foundation of existence.
A continuum that ensures,
every piece of the jigsaw,
fits in the right place,
at the right time.
The flow makes everything possible.
Time was born with the flow,
The universe evolved with the flow.
Galaxies, planets, life,
were all controlled by the flow.
Unnerving and exasperating struggles,
are not worthy of the pain,
if one could only feel,
the feeble nudge of the flow.
The flow is an
unscientific,
insensible,
apparently confusing,
unthoughtful brainchild,

of an overcrowded mind,
coined in a mere flicker of thought.
But who knows?
Maybe the responsible factor,
for the unnecessary notion,
was none other than,
the ever-existing,
flow.

The Anti-Hero

He doesn't believe in principles.
Afterall they are trash.
Just building blocks,
for saddling the free mind.
He doesn't believe in respect.
Afterall it's a fake establishment,
to make it apparent,
to live upto expectations.
He doesn't believe in love,
for it's a binding duty,
to the entire heart, mind and soul.
He doesn't believe in truth,
for he has witnessed,
the honourable and honest,
fall like flies.
He doesn't believe in lies,
for there are none worthy,
of his betrayal of truth.
He doesn't believe in hatred,
for it's useless
and immaterial.
He is just one arrogant and selfish man,
with his,

non-idealistic,

self tailored,

irritating,

obsolete

set of virtues.

Strange Senses

Flowery fragrance,
of laughters.
Sugary sweetness,
in voice,
Blinding beauty,
of behaviour,
Tickling touch,
of thoughts.
Numerous sensations,
Indescribable,
yet mesmerizing.
Like riddles to the brain,
but games for the heart.
Conversations in glances.
Sheepish smiles.
Racing hearts.
Mingling of breaths.
Strange and stupid,
young and dumb,
love.

Hope

A tiny ray of light,
creeping through,
the sharp slit in the roof,
when the soul is locked,
deep inside,
the cellar of insecurities.
Doesn't give much warmth,
but a delicate revival
of the memories of the world beyond the cellar,
of the cherishable opportunities,
of the sweet singing nightingale,
of the cheerful radiance of the sun.
Maybe they are all,
non existent and fictitious,
but the teeny tiny ray,
accomplishes it's purpose.
It energises the halfwitted heart,
if not the logical mind,
that there's still,
some hope.

Heartbreaks

Two souls entwined together,
Reciprocating feelings,
Emotions,
Warmth,
Positivity,
And more than everything trust.
Budding Bonds of Glass,
Weak but full of aspirations,
And then suddenly a deafening crack!
Either one is set aloof,
to mourn the guilt,
to dwell upon mistakes,
to dive in miseries.
The heart forms boundaries,
islanding itself,
setting distances,
for better future.
Biting hopelessness
and engulfed in darkness!
But then the phase slides away,
Waves wash over,
Words engraved in sands,
Cleaning the slate,

Mending the Heart,

And readying it,

for another heartbreak!

Not So Happy Endings

We keep hoping for the best.
Sad endings are
unwanted,
unwelcomed
unpopular.
The world loves it,
When the prince,
rescues the damsel in distress.
When the jungle,
raises a human boy.
When the horrible wolf,
Is killed by the huntsman.
When the malicious witch,
fails to murder an innocent child.
We expect in life,
what we expect from stories.
We hope for the best,
discarding pessimism.
But we forget,
one gruesome policy of the universe-
Ideality never exists.
Things change,
People change,

Situations change,
Times change,
We can't expect
Utmost sincerity,
Immovable honesty,
Unending loyalty,
Unhindered modesty.
There are always,
Broken hearts,
and piercing shards.
We have to learn to
accept,
adapt,
and act.
The nature is a cold-hearted mother.
And so she expects the same out of us!

9 798886 065374

Printed by Libri Plureos GmbH in Hamburg, Germany